21 DAY JUMPSTART

By Josh Jamison

PREFACE

The hardest part of developing any new habit, rhythm or mode of living is always getting started. Whether it's going to the gym, changing your diet or growing closer to God, the first step is usually the hardest step. While the 21 days of Bible reading and reflection outlined here are not a guarantee you'll develop new spiritual habits, it is a great first step to help you get moving in the right direction.

As you look to develop some new patterns in your life, it will be important for you to do more than set alerts, reminders and check things off of your spiritual to-do list. In fact, one of the most important things I've learned about spiritual disciplines is that, often, your posture matters more than the pattern. What I mean by that is the posture of my heart has more impact and influence on what I get out of my spiritual disciplines than the act itself. Let me explain. You can read the Bible every day. You could even read the Bible cover to cover, but if the posture of your heart is not open to receive the truth that is inside of the Bible you will be wasting your time.

This principle permeates every aspect of our spiritual journey because Jesus is not interested in form or religiosity. Instead, He's interested in YOU. He's interested in what is in your heart. He's interested in a real, unfiltered relationship. He wants you to lean in. He wants you to *want* to know Him, not feel obligated to read your daily devotion or attend a service. He wants you to seek Him, to look for him in every line and paragraph as you read scripture. He wants you to sit at His feet, with no rush, hurry or agenda in your voice as you pray to Him. He just wants the two of you to be together. So, as you approach these new patterns you desire to build and develop in your life, make sure you start with your posture. Let your heart be open. Let your expectations be heightened. Let your spirit be ready and let's take the first steps together!

THE BIBLE

What you choose to believe about the Bible matters. It matters because what you choose to believe about the Bible literally impacts every other aspect of your life. What you choose to believe about the Bible shapes your view of God, your view of life, your view of sin, salvation, and Jesus. The Bible has the power to become the lens through which you see your world. I personally choose to believe that the Bible is more than just a collection of stories, but that God himself inspired the writers to pen the words that fill the pages.

This belief dictates how I approach God's word but it also impacts how much say, authority and influence I give the Bible over my life. If the Bible really is God's word, then in my estimation, it requires a position of greater importance and authority in our daily lives. It's my hope and desire that this 21-day jump-start would help you discover the joy and the power of reading scripture and help you experience the reality of who Jesus is and how much He loves you.

PRAYER

God never designed or intended for this journey of following Jesus to be a one-way street of learning head knowledge and participating in organized religion. He desires for us to engage in a two-way relationship that involves conversation, emotion, and intimacy. One of the most profound and powerful gateways of this relationship is through the gift of prayer. Think about this for a moment: God did not *have* to make himself available to us 24 hours a day, 7 days a week, 365 days a year. He didn't owe it to us to give unhindered access to his ear and the ability to interrupt him at any moment with our needs, wants and desires. Even though He didn't have to, He still did.

Out of the overflow of His desire to be with you, He gave you this gift called prayer. This gift literally gives you the ability to call out to Him and in an instant you are no longer just talking to your bedroom wall, you're talking to the King of Kings. Wow! Prayer is more than just reciting form or formulas, and it's certainly much more than just reading a to-do list off to God. Prayer has been given to you as a mechanism for pouring your heart out before God. Sharing with Him your deepest dreams, fears, desires, insecurities, and questions. Taking time to sit and listen, opening your ears and heart to allow Him to speak back to you.

Prayer is the paint that gives the picture of our relationship with God color! It brings it all to life! Without it, we bear the name of Jesus but never fully submit to His Lordship and never fully access the grace, wisdom, and guidance He has made available to us daily. We end up living lives as "Christians" who are, instead of living by His power and grace, living by our own effort and striving.

COMMUNITY

God designed us for relationship. Our primary form of relationship is found in Him, but He also created us to be in a deep, meaningful relationship with one another. One of the greatest gifts Jesus has given us is this gift of a community, a family that we belong to that is held together solely by this bond of faith in Jesus. Like any meaningful relationship in life, if this community Jesus has given us is to work it's going to require effort, patience, grace, and commitment. Effort to live in unity and vulnerability. Patience for the differences we all have. Grace for the ways we will fail one another. Commitment to keep at it even when it's less than perfect.

No church is perfect because it's made up of people. Very broken, flawed and messed up people. One of the greatest ways we undercut this gift of community is by jumping from one community to another every time things don't go our way or every time someone hurts or disappoints us. No plant can survive by being planted, uprooted, re-planted and uprooted over and over. So why do we think we can survive spiritually by doing the same thing in our own lives?

Get planted. Stay planted even when it's hard. It's the only way to grow to the point where you can bear real, lasting fruit the way Jesus designed. So, find a church. Attend regularly. Start serving. Get involved. Get to know people and let them know you, the real you. Commit to stick it out. It might actually become the family that Jesus promised to give you when he adopted you as his child.

DAY 1

Read: Mark 1

Jumpstart devotional: Mark 1:9 *"One day Jesus came from Nazareth in Galilee, and John baptized him in the Jordan River. 10 As Jesus came up out of the water, he saw the heavens splitting apart and the Holy Spirit descending on him like a dove. 11 And a voice from heaven said, "You are my dearly loved Son, and you bring me great joy."* (NLT)

This moment stands out as one of my top five moments in the Bible. I wish I could have witnessed it in person. John baptizes Jesus, and as Jesus comes up out of the water the heavens part, a dove descends on him and they hear the audible voice of God! Wow! One thing I find so compelling about this section of the text is what the Father says about Jesus. He speaks three things over him in one sentence: 1) Identity 2) Affection 3) Affirmation. Identity - You're my son. Affection - I love you. Affirmation - You bring me joy. Just as the Father speaks these three things over Jesus, these are the same things God desires to speak into your heart today! Open your heart and receive this today: You are His child! He loves you with an unconditional love! You bring Him great joy, He delights in you!

Jumpstart questions:

1. What things do I currently find my identity in other than Jesus?

2. Where do I turn to receive affection other than Jesus?

3. Who am I trying to please with the choices I make?

DAY 2

Read: Mark 2

Jumpstart devotional: Mark 2:5 *"Seeing their faith"* (NLT)

These three words are so easy to quickly gloss over in the context of this story, but they carry incredible insight into the heart of Jesus. As Jesus looked he saw the man in need, but what He noted was the faith of the four friends who carried him across town, fought through the crowd, climbed on the roof, broke a hole in the ceiling and risked their reputations as well as their livelihoods all because they believed that one moment with Jesus could change their friend! It was *THAT* faith that stirred the heart of Jesus to do the impossible!

Jumpstart questions:

1.   Do you believe that Jesus has the power to change your friends' lives as he did for the paralyzed man in this story?

2.   If so, what is holding you back from going all in, like these four friends, to get the people in your life to Jesus?

DAY 3

Read: Mark 3

Jumpstart devotional: Mark 3:5 *"He looked around at them angrily and was deeply saddened by their hard hearts." (NLT)*

Jesus doesn't get frustrated with too many people in scripture, but one group he regularly was upset with was the hyper-religious. It wasn't their passion he was frustrated by but, instead, it was the creating of more barriers between people and God that bothered him. Sin is already a big enough barrier between us and God. God doesn't need us creating religious barriers too! Here, Jesus is saddened that they were completely content to allow their list of rules to become a hurdle and barrier between someone who was hurting and God's grace.

Jumpstart questions:

1.   Take a moment and ask the Holy Spirit to reveal anything inside of your heart that is judgmental, stereotypical and prejudice towards others. As He speaks to you and reveals these areas to you, ask Him to heal these areas in your heart.

DAY 4

Read: Psalm 1

Jumpstart devotional: Psalm 1:3 *"They are like trees planted along the riverbank, bearing fruit each season. Their leaves never wither, and they prosper in all they do." (NLT)*

Reading the Bible can quickly and easily become a to-do item that we quickly check off of our daily list. When this happens, reading the Bible becomes a way that we earn God's love instead of spending time in scripture because we recognize that we are already loved by God and we see the Bible as an incredible pathway to get to know Him better and align our lives with Him! The Psalmist reminds us that it's when we approach scripture like this and take the time to meditate on it and commit it to memory, then our lives begin to fully come alive and we can begin to thrive in every season!

Jumpstart questions:

1. How can you begin to take these devotions and Bible reading to the next level in your life?

2. What do you need to do to start the process of memorizing scripture?

DAY 5

Read: Mark 4

Jumpstart devotional: Mark 4:4 *"As he scattered it across his field" (NLT)*

One of the most intriguing parts of this parable of Jesus is that the farmer throws seed everywhere, not just in the soil that he knows will accept the seed. Jesus said the farmer scattered the seed across the entire field which means he was not stingy about sowing seed, but instead was generous and was willing to allow every plot of soil to receive the seed or reject the seed. In this parable, the seed represents the message of grace found in Jesus and you and I are represented by the farmer. The real question Jesus is posing for us is this: Are you willing to share me everywhere and with everyone?

Jumpstart questions:

> 1. Are there any people in your life that you have predetermined would not want to hear about Jesus?
>
> 2. Take a moment and begin to pray for them by name and ask Jesus to give you boldness and courage to be willing to sow the seed of God's grace everywhere and with everyone.

DAY 6

Read: Mark 5

Jumpstart devotional: Mark 5:30 *"Who touched my robe?" (NLT)*

It's pretty amazing that in a crowd of people pressing in around him, one-touch was different than everyone else. It was so different that it stopped Jesus in his tracks. This woman who had a serious issue of bleeding came to Jesus with desperate faith and a deep belief that one touch from Jesus could change everything. This same principle still applies today. You can be in a room where everyone is singing the same songs and listening to the same message, but only a few walk away with a life-changing encounter with God. Why is that?

Jumpstart questions:

      1.   What separated this woman touch from everyone else's touch in the crowd?

      2.   Have you ever come to church and just gone through the motions? Why is that?

DAY 7

Read: Mark 6

Jumpstart devotional: Mark 6:41-44 *"Jesus took the five loaves and two fish, looked up toward heaven, and blessed them. Then, breaking the loaves into pieces, he kept giving the bread to the disciples so they could distribute it to the people. He also divided the fish for everyone to share. They all ate as much as they wanted, and afterward, the disciples picked up twelve baskets of leftover bread and fish. A total of 5,000 men and their families were fed."* (NLT)

What was inadequate in the hands of the disciples became more than enough in the hands of Jesus. The quantity didn't change, but the hands holding the loaves and fish did. I know this may not seem like a new revelation but in the hands of Jesus, anything is possible. As we look at our lives the reality is that we are inadequate in many ways. Left to ourselves we cannot measure up to meet our own needs, let alone the needs of those around us. But when we place our lives (our gifts, talents, abilities, etc.) in the hands of Jesus, He can use us to do things we were never capable of doing on our own!

Jumpstart questions:

1.   Take some personal inventory of your life. Have you put every part of your life in Jesus' hands? Your relationships, your dreams, your fears, etc.?

2.   If the answer is no, what is stopping you from taking that step right now?

DAY 8

Read: Proverbs 3

Jumpstart devotional: Proverbs 3:5-6 *"Trust in the Lord with all your heart; do not depend on your own understanding. Seek his will in all you do, and he will show you which path to take." (NLT)*

It's estimated that the average person makes somewhere around 35,000 decisions a day. They are mostly small and non-consequential choices, but how can we seek God's will in such a rapid-fire and reactionary world? This doesn't mean that we have to stop and ask God what side of the bed to get out of or which shoe which should put on first. Instead, the way we live this out is by learning and discovering the heart and character of God and shaping our will to match His will the best we can. The more He changes us from the inside out the more our big and small choices alike will align with His heart.

Jumpstart questions:

1. Do you stop and ask God what He wants when you're making big decisions or do you just trust your gut?

2. How can you begin to allow God's heart to shape how you make your everyday decisions, big and small?

DAY 9

Read: Mark 7

Jumpstart devotional: Mark 7:15 *"It's not what goes into your body that defiles you; you are defiled by what comes from your heart." (NLT)*

As Jesus is specifically speaking to the dietary restrictions of the old covenant and the way that the religious rulers were using it, he paints a picture for us about real purity. Too often we ask the question "How far can I go before it's sin?". This sort of thinking is fixated on pushing the limit. Instead, Jesus challenges us to see how close we can get our heart to his heart instead of focusing on how close we can get to sin and not get burned.

Jumpstart questions:

    1.   What is an area of your life that you have been living too close to the edge of sin?

    2.   Who do you need to tell about this struggle so you can begin to develop accountability and new standards in this area?

DAY 10

Read: Mark 8

Jumpstart devotional: Mark 8:24-25 *"The man looked around. "Yes," he said, "I see people, but I can't see them very clearly. They look like trees walking around." Then Jesus placed his hands on the man's eyes again, and his eyes were opened. His sight was completely restored, and he could see everything clearly." (NLT)*

It's easy to read the gospels and get used to the instantaneous nature of many of Jesus' miracles. However, here we find a different kind of encounter. This was a miracle that wasn't instantaneous but was a process. Sometimes God's answer leads us on a journey. The journey may be moments, months or years. Often, it's in the moments of waiting where God does the deepest miracles, He deals with the issues in our hearts.

Jumpstart questions:

     1.   Think of a time when you felt like God didn't answer your prayer right away? What did you learn from that journey?

     2.   Did God making you wait change how you viewed God's goodness or faithfulness? How?

DAY 11

Read: Mark 9

Jumpstart devotional: Mark 9:35 *"Whoever wants to be first must take last place and be the servant of everyone else." (NLT)*

Greatness in our culture is often depicted as achievement, incredible success, and popularity. It's wealth, fame and notoriety. Jesus flipped that narrative on its head when He teaches us about greatness in the kingdom of God. It's not about making a name for yourself or trying to achieve success. Greatness in the kingdom of God looks a lot like serving, loving and sacrificing. It is putting the needs of others before your own. Sounds a lot like Jesus, doesn't it?

Jumpstart questions:

    1.   What would have to happen for you to naturally think of the needs of others before yourself?

    2.   What next steps do you need to take today to start this process in your life?

DAY 12

Read: Mark 10

Jumpstart devotional: Mark 10:22 *"At this, the man's face fell, and he went away sad, for he had many possessions." (NLT)*

I once heard it said that "It's okay for you to have possessions. You just can't allow your possessions to have you." It's a simple, yet profound idea. The man's face fell and he went away sad, not because he had so many possessions, but because his possessions had his heart. Whatever has possession of your heart can lead, guide and direct your life however it chooses.

Jumpstart questions:

    1.   What currently has your heart, honestly? What is the greatest influence on your choices, decisions, and desires?

    2.   Take a moment and pray. Ask the Holy Spirit to reveal what is currently holding your heart. Pray that God would help you surrender your whole heart to him.

DAY 13

Read: Psalm 15

Jumpstart devotional: Psalm 15:2-3 *"Those who lead blameless lives and do what is right, speaking the truth from sincere hearts. Those who refuse to gossip or harm their neighbors or speak evil of their friends." (NLT)*

There's a difference between being around the things of God and experiencing them deeply and personally for yourself. One of the determining factors is the posture and position of your heart. Much of it has to do with your actions, but God pays special attention to what comes out of your mouth. It's out of the overflow of your heart that your mouth speaks. This is why the Psalmist notes the importance of speaking the truth, refusing to gossip or speaking evil of your friends. Your mouth is an outward expression of your inward condition.

Jumpstart questions:

1.   If someone were to take an inventory of what you say over a week, how much evidence would there be of God in your life?

2.   Think for a moment about an area of your speech that needs to grow? Do you struggle with profanity, lying, gossip, sarcasm, etc.? Whatever it may be for you, talk to God about it, but also find a leader in your youth ministry to talk to. We grow when we have real and authentic accountability with people who genuinely know and care about us.

DAY 14

Read: Mark 11

Jumpstart devotional: Mark 11:17 *"He said to them, "The Scriptures declare, 'My Temple will be called a house of prayer for all nations,' but you have turned it into a den of thieves." (NLT)*

Jesus is referring to the temple here in Mark 11 but the truth is that we turn the church into a lot of things that Jesus never intended for it to be. If we're not careful we can make God's house a social club, a clique, our religious duty, routine and ordinary. Jesus didn't die on the cross so you could fill a seat on a Sunday. He died on the cross to give you so much more than a service to attend. He died to give you a family you could belong to. Let's never take God's house for granted or turn it into something Jesus never designed for it to be.

Jumpstart questions:

1.   When you think of "Church" what is the first thing that comes to your mind? Why?
2.   What do you look forward to the most about going to church?
3.   What do you think God looks forward to the most about you going to church?

DAY 15

Read: Mark 12

Jumpstart devotional: Mark 12:28 *"Of all the commandments, which is the most important?" (NLT)*

Wow! Talk about a loaded question! Here, amid teachers of the religious law trying to trip him up, Jesus gives a powerful and simple answer to such a loaded question. What is his summary answer? Love God & love people. While this may not seem like a revolutionary statement, the fact that Jesus placed loving God at an equal level of importance with loving your neighbor should cause us all to stop for a moment. You can do all the right "religious" stuff, but if you fail at loving others it doesn't matter.

Jumpstart questions:

1.   Have you viewed loving others as important as loving God? Why or why not?

2.   Why do you think this was such a big deal to Jesus?

DAY 16

Read: Mark 13

Jumpstart devotional: Mark 13:33 *"And since you don't know when that time will come, be on guard! Stay alert!" (NLT)*

With every generation, we tend to swing the pendulum to the opposite extreme of how we were raised. When I was growing up it seemed like people were obsessed with the rapture. Best-selling books were written about it, movies made about it, it was even used as a scare tactic to get you to behave. I mean, you don't want to be left behind, do you? Honestly, in our pendulum swinging ways, we probably don't talk about this reality enough: Jesus is coming back. This is a real thing. He's coming back. Instead of this idea conjuring fear, it should illicit expectation and urgency in our lives. If Jesus is really coming back: every moment counts, every conversation matters! I'm not worried about being left behind I'm worried about those who might be left behind if we don't share Jesus with them.

Jumpstart questions:

1.   If you knew that Jesus was coming back today, what would you do differently?
2.   What is stopping you from living every day like that?

DAY 17

Read: Proverbs 12

Jumpstart devotional: Proverbs 12:15 *"Fools think their own way is right, but the wise listen to others." (NLT)*

The video game Goldeneye 007 on Nintendo 64 was one of the first games I ever played where your perspective on the screen was through the eyes of your character. This was known as a "First Person Shooter" game. As cool as the visual experience seemed, there was one thing that always drove me nuts: I could only see from one perspective! It was always hard to see what was going on around me. This is so true about our lives today, and this is exactly what Solomon is referring to in Proverbs 12. When left to our limited perspective, we don't see the whole picture. We are blinded by our own biases and motives. Instead, we need others in our lives who can help us have a well-rounded vantage point to see all sides of the situations and circumstances we are facing.

Jumpstart questions:

    1.   Who is someone in your life that you seek counsel from?

    2.   Are they the kind of person who is going to tell you the truth or just what you want to hear?

DAY 18

Read: Mark 14

Jumpstart devotional: Mark 14:36 *"Abba, Father,"* he cried out, *"everything is possible for you. Please take this cup of suffering away from me. Yet I want your will to be done, not mine." (NLT)*

What a powerful and profound moment. Here we see Jesus, beginning to feel the weight and burden of our sin, actually ask the Father if there is any other way to carry out this mission other than having to die on the cross. It's a real and raw picture of the humanity of Jesus. He knew what he was about to endure. In the midst of it all, Jesus adds on one powerful and qualifying statement: "Yet I want Your will to be done, not mine". What Jesus just expressed to the Father is the same sentiment that you and I need to carry in our own hearts. At the end of the day, it doesn't matter what I want, the only thing that should matter is what God wants.

Jumpstart questions:

    1.   Are you willing to trust God even when what he's asking you to do is hard and uncomfortable?

    2.   Think of what the most difficult thing you've had to go through has been. How did God help you through it?

DAY 19

Read: Mark 15

Jumpstart devotional: Mark 15:37-38 *"Then Jesus uttered another loud cry and breathed his last. And the curtain in the sanctuary of the Temple was torn in two, from top to bottom." (NLT)*

This curtain was not like your grandma's curtains that she knit together before you were born. This curtain was made of leather and was over a foot thick! It separated the temple workers from the "Holy of Holies" but even more importantly, it also separated the people from the presence of God. When Jesus breathed his last breath and the earth shook this curtain wasn't torn by accident. It was a symbol. The presence of God that was once reserved for a few was now available to all because of the work that Jesus did when he died on the cross for our sins!

Jumpstart questions:

1. How often would you say you access or try to reach out to God every day?

2. If Jesus' death on the cross not only forgave your sins but gave you access to God, how often do you think Jesus wants you to take advantage of that opportunity?

DAY 20

Read: Mark 16

Jumpstart devotional: Mark 16:15 *"And then he told them, "Go into all the world and preach the Good News to everyone." (NLT)*

This moment is referred to as the "Great Commission". A commission is defined as an authorization or command. Notice, it's not a recommendation or option. Often, we treat many aspects of our Christian faith as optional requests that we can opt-in or opt-out of depending on how we feel about it. However, this commission to share the Gospel with the world is not a casual ask, it's an urgent command. The time we have here on earth is short, every moment counts, every person counts.

Jumpstart questions:

    1. What needs to change for you to begin living every day with a sense of urgency around this "commission" from Jesus?

    2. What part of sharing your faith with others scares you the most? Why?

DAY 21

Read: Psalm 51

Jumpstart devotional: Psalm 51:17 *"The sacrifice you desire is a broken spirit. You will not reject a broken and repentant heart, O God." (NLT)*

Repentance is not a popular or warm and fuzzy word. It can often evoke tones of pain, heartache and discipline. However, at its core, repentance is a simple term to signify a change of direction. God isn't just looking for you to change your behavior. He's looking for you to change the direction of your heart. To turn your heart from the direction of selfishness, self-sufficiency, and independence and turn your heart towards him!

Jumpstart questions:

    1.   What direction is your heart currently aiming? What is holding you back from turning your heart fully and completely to Jesus?

    2.   What behaviors have you been trying to change that may require you to dig deeper into the condition and position of your heart?

CONCLUSION

I hope these last few weeks have helped you grow closer to Jesus and develop a love for spending time in scripture. As you take your next steps it will be so important for you to continue in this daily discipline of reading scripture, spending time in prayer and being rooted in community. Some great tips to help you would be:

- Download the YouVersion Bible App and pick a Bible reading plan to start this week.

- Follow a playlist of worship music and start filling your day with praise.

- Find a local church and start attending. If you already have a local church, dive into a small group or start serving in an area of ministry.

These things are not an all-inclusive list but they are a great place to continue this journey! Remember, this journey of following Jesus is a marathon, not a sprint. There will be moments where you feel tired, worn out and ready to quit. People will disappoint you, some parts of your devotions will feel dry and you may struggle to maintain consistency. My encouragement to you is this: Don't quit! Don't give up! Keep going! The journey you are on is worth it!